Spiders Up Close

Robin Birch

Chicago, Illinois

© 2005 Raintree

Published by Raintree, a division of Reed Elsevier, Inc.

Chicago, Illinois

Customer Service 888-363-4266

Visit our website at www.raintreelibrary.com

For information, address the publisher:
Raintree, 100 N. LaSalle, Suite 1200, Chicago, IL 60602

09 08 07 06 05
10 9 8 7 6 5 4 3 2 1

Printed and bound in Hong Kong and China by WKT Company Limited.

Library of Congress Cataloging-in-Publication Data

Birch, Robin.
   Spiders up close / Robin Birch.
      p. cm. -- (Minibeasts up close)
   Includes bibliographical references (p. 30).
   ISBN 1-4109-1142-X -- ISBN 1-4109-1149-7
   1. Spiders--Juvenile literature. I. Title. II. Series: Birch, Robin. Minibeasts up close.
   QL458.4.B57 2004
   595.4--dc22

                                2004003113

Acknowledgments
The publisher would like to thank the following for permission to reproduce photographs:
p. 4 OSF/photolibrary.com; p. 5 Steven David Miller/ Goetgheluck/ Auscape; p. 6 Ken Griffiths/ANT Photo Library; p. 7 Greg Harold/ Goetgheluck/Auscape; pp. 8, 26 Photo Researchers/photolibrary. com; p. 10 C. Andrew Henley/Goetgheluck/Auscape; pp. 11, 25 (bottom) Jiri Lochman/ Lochman Transparencies; pp. 12, 18 Animals Animals/photolibrary.com; pp. 13, 27, 28 Paul Zborowski; p. 14 ANT Jim Frazier/Photo Library; p. 15 Otto Rogge/ANT Photo Library; p. 16 Jay Sarson/Lochman Transparencies; pp. 17, 19 SPL/ photolibrary.com; p. 19 Pho.n.e./Goetgheluck/Auscape; p. 22 Andrew Davoll/Lochman Transparencies; p. 23 Mike Gray/Nature Focus; p. 24 Cyril Webster/ANT Photo Library ; p. 25 (top) Stanley Breeden/Lochman Transparencies; p. 29 Index Stock/photolibrary.com.

Cover photograph of a red-back spider reproduced with permission of Jiri Lochman/Lochman Transparencies.

Every effort has been made to contact copyright holders of any material reproduced in this book. Any omissions will be rectified in subsequent printings if notice is given to the publisher.

Contents

Any words appearing in bold, **like this,** are explained in the Glossary.

Amazing Spiders!

Have you seen a spider lately? Have you seen one on a web? Have you wondered what spiders do all day? Spiders are amazing when you get to know them close up.

Spiders are not insects. They do not have feelers or wings.

What are spiders?

Spiders belong to a group of animals called arachnids. Arachnids are animals with eight legs. A spider has a thin, hard skin called an **exoskeleton** on the outside of its body, instead of bones inside its body.

There are about 35,000 different kinds, or **species,** of spiders. The largest spiders have bodies about as long as a computer mouse. The smallest spiders are smaller than the head of a pin.

Some spiders build webs to catch insects for food.

Bird-eating spiders

The largest spiders are the Goliath bird-eating spiders. They hunt at night for mice, frogs, lizards, and small birds.

5

Where Do Spiders Live?

Spiders live in all parts of the world, except Antarctica. They live in all kinds of **habitats**, including forests, deserts, and mountains.

Most spiders eat insects, so spiders live wherever there are insects. Some spiders live in trees and bushes. Some live in the soil, or under stones, rocks, bark, or wood. Other spiders live in buildings.

Trapdoor spiders build burrows, or holes, with a trapdoor lid over the entrance.

Bird dung spiders

Bird dung spiders look like bird droppings. Their **cephalothoraxes** and **abdomens** are the same color as a bird dropping, and they have a lumpy shape. This protects them from **predators** such as birds, which do not notice them.

Camouflage

Many spiders have shapes, colors, and patterns that make them look like they are part of the place where they live. For example, they may be the same color as the tree trunk they live on. This is called camouflage.

Camouflage protects spiders from animals that might want to eat them. It can also hide them from their **prey** when they are hunting.

This spider has camouflage that makes it look like a flower.

Spider Body Parts

A spider's body has two parts. The first part is made of the head and chest joined together. It is called the **cephalothorax.** The second part is called the **abdomen.**

palps

jaw

cephalothorax

eight eyes

abdomen

spinneret

The cephalothorax

A spider's mouthparts and eyes are on the head part of its cephalothorax. Its mouthparts are the mouth, **jaws,** and **palps.** There are eight legs joined to the cephalothorax.

The abdomen

On many spiders, the abdomen is larger than the cephalothorax. The abdomen is like a bag. It swells up when it is full of food or eggs. Spiders make silk threads that come out of special tubes at the end of the abdomen called **spinnerets.**

The exoskeleton

The **exoskeleton** keeps the spider's shape and stops it from being hurt easily. It also traps water inside the spider's body to keep it from drying out. The exoskeleton is covered with hairs.

Spider Mouthparts

A spider has a small mouth underneath its head. On the front of the head it has two **jaws.** On the end of each jaw is a sharp **fang.** Each fang has a tiny tube in it. **Venom** passes down the tube and through a hole near the end of the fang.

Spitting spiders

Spitting spiders spit glue from their fangs. These small spiders can squirt glue the length of a new pencil eraser. They stick down their prey with the glue before biting it.

Spiders bite **prey** with their fangs.

fangs

Palps

A spider has a **palp,** like a finger, on each side of its jaws. The two palps feel and hold food. On some spiders they are quite large, and look like short legs.

The palps have rows of small teeth for chewing prey. The teeth are located near where the palps attach to the head.

A spider uses its palps to move food to its mouth.

Fangs and Eating

Spiders drink liquids, usually from inside insects. Some spiders eat other small animals as well, such as frogs and mice.

Venom

When a spider catches its **prey,** it bites with its **fangs. Venom** runs down through the fangs and goes into the animal. The venom stops the prey from moving. It comes from venom **glands** in the spider's head.

Almost all spiders use venom to catch and kill their prey.

Mashing and sucking

The spider then lets liquids out
of glands in its upper lip. The
liquids go into the prey and make it
mushy. The spider then crushes and
mashes up the prey with its **jaws** and **palps.**

When the prey is mashed up and juicy, the spider
sucks it up through its mouth. The spider's mouth
is very small, so it can only drink liquids.

Crab spiders

Crab spiders do not
mash up their prey like
other spiders. They bite
insects with their fangs
and then suck liquid out
through the bite holes.

**This spider is using its palps and jaws to crush
its prey before sucking up the liquids.**

Eight Eyes for Seeing

Most spiders have eight eyes. They are usually in two rows on top of their heads. There is a front, lower row and a back, upper row of eyes.

A spider can see up close with some of its eyes. With its other eyes a spider sees dark and light, and movement in the distance.

Wolf spiders have good eyesight. They have four smaller eyes in front and four larger eyes arranged in a square shape on top of their heads.

How well do spiders see?

Most spiders do not see very well. Spiders that live in dark places, or catch their **prey** in webs, do not need to see well. They rely mostly on touch and smell to know what is happening around them. Some spiders that live in dark caves do not even have eyes.

Net-casting spider

A net-casting spider has two huge eyes so it can see insects at night. It holds a web net between its front feet. When it sees an insect coming, it swoops down with its net.

small eye

large eye

Hairs for Sensing

Spiders **sense** with their hairs and feet, and by feeling **vibrations.**

Sensing with hairs

Spiders have hairs all over their bodies. They can touch, taste, and hear things with their hairs. Some of the hairs are very thin and stand up straight. These hairs pick up very small movements of the air around the spider. Some hairs taste by touching.

Tasting hairs are spread all over the spider's body.

Sensing with feet

A spider uses tiny holes on its feet to smell things. Its feet also can feel whether the air is damp or dry.

Sensing vibrations

A spider feels movement with tiny slits all over its **exoskeleton.** These help a web-building spider feel vibrations made by an insect caught in its web. When it senses the insect, the spider rushes over and catches it.

This is a highly magnified view of a spider's foot, showing the sensing hairs.

Sensing each other

Spiders **communicate** with each other. They may make vibrations, such as tapping on a leaf, or a web, or water. Some spiders make sounds to communicate by rubbing parts of their bodies together. Spiders often touch and stroke each other. They see and smell each other, too.

Eight Legs for Moving

Spiders can walk and run. Some spiders can jump. Each of a spider's eight legs has seven sections, including the foot. The legs have hairs and **spines** on them.

Web-building spiders

Spiders that catch their **prey** in webs have three claws on the end of each foot. They use these claws to hold on to the web and their prey.

A spider has eight legs joined to its **cephalothorax.**

Hunting spiders

Spiders that hunt their
prey have two claws on the end
of each foot. These claws have
tiny teeth on them.

Jumping spiders

Jumping spiders catch their
prey by jumping on them.
Some can jump more than
50 times the length of their
bodies. They push off with
their four back legs.

Hunting spiders also can have many tiny hairs under
their feet. These hairs help hold the spider's feet down
if they are walking on a smooth or damp surface.
They also help the spider hold its prey.

Spiders have
claws on the
end of each foot
for gripping.

Outside and Inside a Spider

A hard shell covers the back of a spider's **cephalothorax.** The skin on the **abdomen** is soft.

The heart

A spider has a long, thin heart running down the middle of its abdomen. The heart pumps blood around the body.

How do spiders get air?

Many spiders have lungs. These take in air through a hole called a **spiracle.** The spiracle is on the bottom of the spider. Some spiders have tiny tubes that take air into the body through spiracles.

What happens to food?

A spider's food goes from the **sucking stomach** to the food stomach to be **digested.** Waste passes out of the **anus** as droppings.

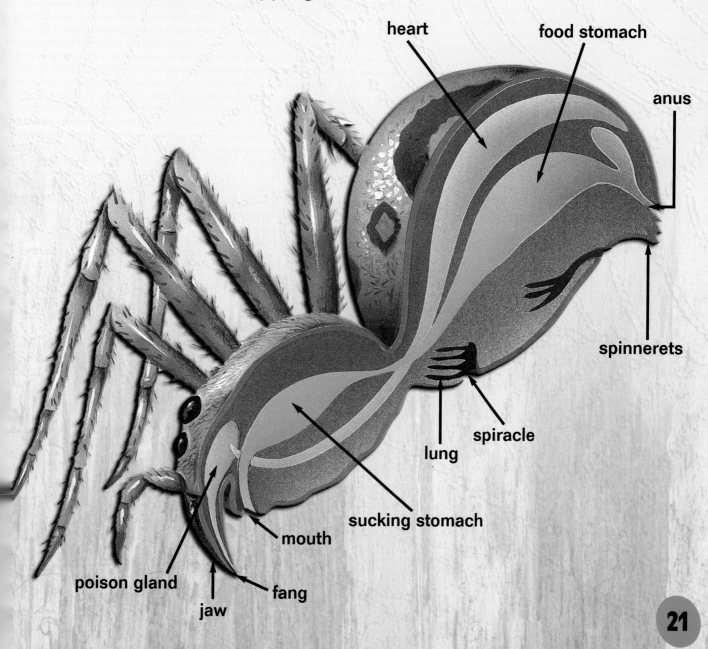

heart

food stomach

anus

spinnerets

spiracle

lung

sucking stomach

mouth

fang

poison gland

jaw

Making Silk

All spiders make silk. Spider silk is stronger than steel wire of the same thickness.

A spider makes silk in **glands** in its **abdomen.** Most spiders have three pairs of **spinnerets** at the end of the abdomen. The spinnerets have tiny tubes in them. These tubes make different kinds of silk.

Threads of silk come out of the spinnerets on the abdomen.

What is silk for?

Many spiders build webs with their silk. Spiders also use silk to wrap up their **prey,** to make nests, and to wrap up their eggs. They can also spin out a thread of silk behind them. They use this thread to drop down from wherever they are.

Ballooning

Some **spiderlings** spin threads of silk and fly in the air with them. This is called ballooning. In summer, the air can be full of spiderlings' silk.

A spider makes different kinds of silk for different uses. Some silk is dry and some is sticky.

Spinning a Web

Different spiders make different kinds of webs to catch food. Webs may be round or fluffy. Others are like sheets. Some spiders make nets, and some make traps.

Orb spiders

Orb spiders make round webs by building spokes from the center, like the spokes of a wheel. Then they go around and around the spokes, leaving silk behind them to finish the web. The silk is sticky to catch insects.

bolas

Bolas spiders

Bolas spiders spin
a silk thread with a ball of
sticky silk on the end called a bolas. They twirl the
bolas around when they sense a flying insect is near.

Black house spiders

Black house spiders build
tangled webs in the corners of
windows or inside buildings.
The web may have a cone-
shaped section where the
spider hides. Insects get
tangled in these webs.

Life Cycle of Spiders

Spiders hatch from eggs. A female spider **mates** with a male, and then she lays her eggs.

Tiny spiders might lay only one egg. Larger spiders may lay more than 1,000 eggs. The female builds a silk egg bag around the eggs, and the young spiders start to grow inside. The eggs usually hatch after a few days or weeks. The young spiders are called **spiderlings.**

This egg bag has been opened to show the eggs and spiderlings inside.

Molting

When the spiders grow too big for their skin, the skin splits open and they climb out. This is called molting. Spiders molt several times as they grow into adults.

This growing spider (below) is shedding its skin (above) for a new and bigger one.

Spiders and Us

Many people are afraid of spiders. This may be because of the way they look. It also may be because spiders can move very suddenly.

Can spiders hurt us?

Most spiders will try to run and hide if they are upset. Only a few will try to defend themselves.

Most spiders do not bite people. Most of them cannot even break human skin because their **fangs** are too short. A few spiders can kill people because their **venom** is poisonous to people.

Spiders catch insects that spread disease. This spider has caught a fly.

The next time you see a spider, remember that it is probably just looking for something to eat.

Useful spiders

Indoors, spiders catch pests such as flies and mosquitoes. Outdoors, they catch insects that eat garden plants. Spiders are also useful to the animals that eat them!

Find Out for Yourself

You may be able to find a spider and its web, inside or outdoors. Are there insects caught in the web? Watch the spider and see what it does.

Books to read

Allan, Tony and David Jefferis. *Spider*. Chicago: Raintree, 2001.

Gareth Stevens Publishing Staff. *Spiders*. Milwaukee: Gareth Stevens, 2004.

Morgan, Sally. *Spiders*. Irvine, Calif.: QEB Publishing, 2004.

Using the Internet

Explore the Internet to find more about spiders. Have an adult help you use a search engine. Type in a keyword such as *spiders,* or the name of a particular spider.

Glossary

abdomen last of the two main sections of a spider

anus hole in the abdomen through which droppings pass

cephalothorax spider's body part made of head and chest joined together

communicate send and receive messages

digest break down food so an animal can use it for energy and growth

exoskeleton hard outside skin of a spider

fang pointed tooth

gland part of body that makes something for a special use, such as venom or silk

habitat place where an animal or plant lives

jaw hard mouthpart used for biting and holding food

mate when a male and a female come together to produce young

palp small body part like a finger, near a spider's mouth

predator animal that kills and eats another animal

prey animal that is caught and eaten by another animal

sense how an animal knows what is going on around it, such as by hearing, seeing, or smelling

species type or kind of animal; animals of the same species can produce young together

spiderling very young spider

spine hard, pointed spike

spinneret body part on the end of a spider's abdomen through which silk passes out

spiracle tiny air hole on a spider's body that lets air inside

sucking stomach stomach that sucks in a spider's food

venom poison

vibration fast, shaking movement

31

Index